Contemporary Crafts

Frames
and
Framing

Barbara Dizdar

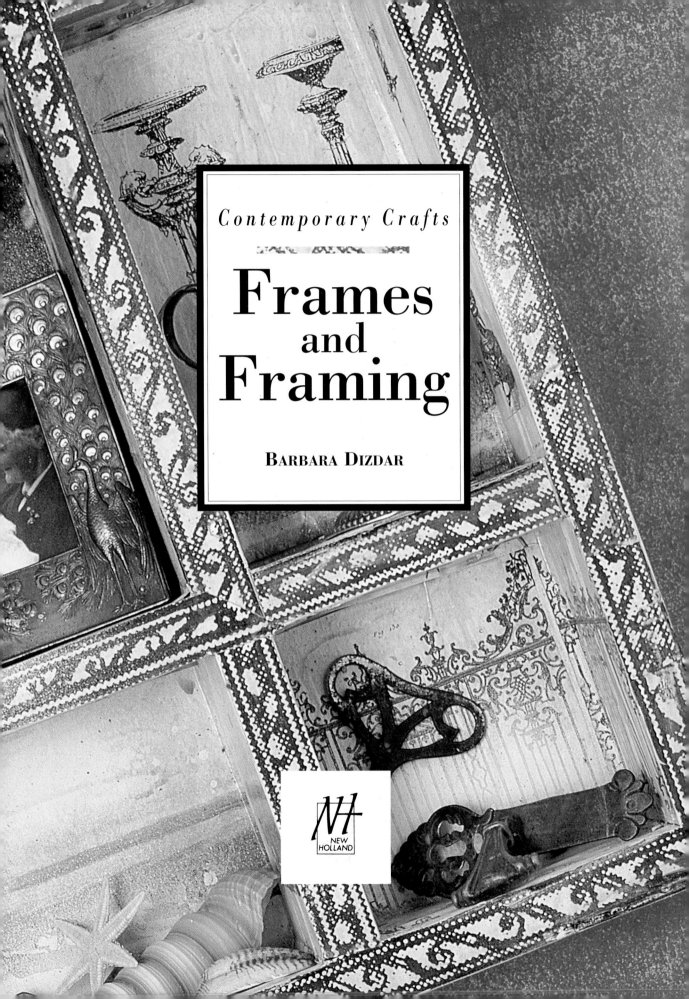

Contemporary Crafts

Frames
and
Framing

Barbara Dizdar

NH
NEW
HOLLAND

For Tihomir Dizdar

First published in 1996 by
New Holland (Publishers) Ltd
London • Cape Town • Sydney • Singapore

24 Nutford Place
London W1H 6DQ
United Kingdom

80 McKenzie Street
Cape Town 8001
South Africa

3/2 Aquatic Drive
Frenchs Forest, NSW 2086
Australia

ISBN 1 85368 683 2 (hbk)
ISBN 1 85368 844 4 (pbk)

Editor: Coral Walker
Designer: Paul Cooper
Photographer: Jason Lowe
Managing Editor: Gillian Haslam

Acknowledgements
A big thank you to everyone at Dizar. Also to Simonart of London E2 for their help and loan of
materials; Tempus Stet Ltd of London SE16 for the photograph on page 8; Wilde at Art, London SW6
for the loan of their beautiful mirrors; Principia Press, 204 Jamaica Road, London SE16 4RT for the print on
page 9; Bombay Duck, 16 Malton Road, London W10 5UP for the metal canisters and wooden fish
on page 30; The Pine Shop in London NW6 for their help, Mat at Camden Lock Market for his
Egyptian-style papyrus and to Coral and Jason for all their support.

Reproduction by Hirt and Carter, Cape Town, South Africa
Printed and bound in Singapore by Tien Wah Press (Pte) Ltd

C ONTENTS

INTRODUCTION

FRAMES HAVE EXISTED in one form or another across every civilisation for centuries. A frame gives importance and power to the image within, drawing the eye and holding the viewer's attention. In *Frames and Framing*, I have tried to show the various ways in which an image can be framed, taking inspiration from history, crafts and from the imagination.

Decorative painted borders are perhaps the first kind of frame. The most basic 'frame' surely is to take the floor as the first horizontal, the ceiling as the second, and to create the vertical lines with pillars. This creates an area to view within four borders. Many cultures experimented with this concept. Egyptian panels use lotus trees as vertical lines, and early frescoes often created alcoves: arched tops with two pillars on either side. Early illuminated manuscripts surrounded the writing with decorative and ornamental borders to give dignity to the manuscript and inspire the reader.

Places of worship were important homes for great works of art and were the only place most common people would see any paintings. The importance of these works of art was therefore crucial: they had to inspire worship, evoke a spiritual life to which the observer should aspire, and provide a respite from the brutal or mundane reality of daily life. The borders

This arched mirror reflects the baroque style of the great houses of Europe; it is made to look old and faded with various paint techniques.

. . . .

around these images therefore had to reflect the same sentiments, and so the early 'frames' become beautifully ornamental.

The frame as an object developed with the need for mobility. The traditional frescoes were permanently fixed to the walls, but religious belief was subject to quick changes. As western civilisations fought over religion, their icons had to be moved and displayed elsewhere.

The triptych was one frame designed specifically with transport in mind. A beautiful gold leaf Madonna could be safely transported in its own hinged 'box', the two doors folding out to reveal other saints or religious images on the panels on either side. As the icons grew in importance, so did their frames.

As painters began to be recognised as artists and not simply artisans, vast sums of money began to be spent on commissions. Canvas and oil paint allowed work to be portable, and so paintings began to be seen in terms of possessions. These acquisitions were expensive and needed to be shown as such. Wealthy men would achieve recognition by having their portraits painted by a great royal court painter or one of his followers. These same men would lend their patronage to the church to ensure the preservation both of their reputations and their souls. Frames not only served the purpose of directing the eye, they also ensured that everyone knew this was a valuable possession.

So frames developed to inspire awe and splendour. Magnificently carved and gilded frames became a necessity for a painting. The

A Regency-style caryatid recreated by Tempus Stet. Its reflection reveals wall-to-wall frames which were also fashionable at the time.

. . . .

royal courts and country homes of Europe were filled with wooden, silver and china frames made by the greatest crafts people of the times.

As royalty and gentry competed with each other for fine things, frames became something of a status symbol. Louis XIV of France had a mirror frame made from slabs of agate and precious stones. The overall effect is sumptuous and reflects the exuberant style of a monarch dedicated to decadence.

From wood carvers to stone masons, from gilders to china manufacturers, each trade perfected their techniques in making frames. A huge array of pictures, mirrors and reliefs now adorned the walls of the rich. As fashion was directed from the top, gilded and decorated frames became standard throughout the upper classes. The greater your position in life, the more ornate the frame.

Up until and throughout the 19th century, frames were still highly decorative. But as the middle classes grew, smaller frames became more popular. More people took to producing their own work and watercolours and portraits were widely available. By the late 19th century it became fashionable to cover the walls with frames: the quality of the work inside being of little importance compared to the overall view. Photography became widespread and portraiture was available to many. All these portraits needed to be displayed, so frames grew in abundance.

Then in the 1930s, art deco introduced a simpler, more linear style. Decorative art nouveau curves were replaced by straight lines. The architects of the Bauhaus removed any unnecessary appendages to the house: many removed frames all together. Pictures were simply wrapped around the stretchers or placed behind glass. The decorative form was severely questioned. These modernists challenged classicism and tradition and, in returning to function and form, they created the atmosphere for the 20th century.

Throughout this century, the artist has had the opportunity to experiment. When considering a frame, it is possible to see it not merely as a pretext of conveying the impression of wealth and position, but to look at the frame as a vehicle of expression. Just as the craftsman attempted to execute finer and more intricate skills to his art, the artist or designer can now use the frame and the image in tandem to express their own creativity. It is possible to be pure or splendid, decorative or minimalist.

Influences on framing today come from across the world. With an ever widening trade in goods between Europe, Asia, Africa and the Americas, we are able to experience styles and designs from other cultures.

As part of a series on contemporary crafts, I have tried to point out in this book that we now have the licence to experiment. There are so many textures, shapes and designs available, we can take the widest view of framing.

The basic steps will teach you to make the simplest frame. If you are framing a picture it may be all you need to know, but even at this stage, there is an enormous range of mouldings available from which to choose. You must ask yourself what you want at this most basic level: varnished or waxed hardwoods provide beautiful borders for old or new pictures. Some softwoods will also be enhanced by a colour wash. A whitewash of paint creates a summery, sun-bleached look. Bright coloured stains can make an impact with strongly coloured prints. Classical moulding in gilt or carved wood will add splendour and weight to oil paintings or classical prints. Etchings, lithographs, or other fine prints look good with simple white mounts and narrow frames, focussing the eye on a line drawing rather than distracting it with a busy border. However, there should be no hard and

An 18th century Chippendale chimney piece displays an elaborate ornamental 'frame'.

. . . .

This Egyptian-inspired painting on papyrus shows the ancient and instinctive desire to 'frame' an image.

. . . .

fast rules, it is important to look at the image, to look at the space it will be hung in and to decide accordingly.

Personally, I like to play with historical splendour. I use experimental textures, such as fabric and lace, goblets and statues, so that it is possible to recreate some of the opulence of traditional frames using non-traditional methods and materials. Whether you want to make a frame from scratch, or simply decorate one you have bought, this book will show you how. In the projects that follow, I have illustrated techniques, textures and media which may not be immediately obvious but which I hope you can then mould and adapt with your own imagination and inspiration.

MATERIALS AND EQUIPMENT

TO MAKE A FRAME, you only need to spend a small amount of money: a mitre block, wood glue, a saw and some nails. However, there is equipment on the market that helps to ensure straight cuts, seamless corners and good right-angled frames. We list the simpler materials and equipment you need, along with a few more expensive items. Allow yourself plenty of time and find a place to work which gives you enough room.

FRAMING

MITRE BLOCK A traditional piece of equipment which is used in conjunction with a tenon saw to create accurate 45 degree cuts. This is vital when creating a traditional square or rectangular frame as you must ensure the moulding is cut precisely. A mitre block is not very expensive and is available from most hardware or DIY stores. You will also need a piece of 5 x 2.5 cm (2 x 1 in) scrap timber to put inside the block when sawing your moulding.

TENON SAW Although any ordinary hand saw will suffice, a tenon saw is recommended for use in a mitre block as it is sturdier and will give you more control.

WOODEN MOULDINGS These form the basis of most traditional square or rectangular frames. There are many stockists of mouldings. For the widest selection, contact a framing specialist, although timber merchants, some builders' merchants and DIY stores stock mouldings, and it is worth finding somewhere which stocks a wide selection and sells small quantities. If you can obtain a catalogue of mouldings, it is fun to browse through this at your leisure in the comfort of your own home.

HAND DRILL Small drills are available for intricate work, but a standard hand drill can be used for framing. If the drill bits are too large, you can cut the headings off moulding pins and use these instead.

MOULDING PINS OR VENEER PINS These are better than panel pins as they are sharper and thinner and they will not split the frame when you hammer them in place.

WOOD ADHESIVE Used for gluing mouldings together, white PVA based wood adhesive is available from hardware and DIY stores.

HAMMER Choose a middleweight hammer. Anything too heavy will probably be difficult to handle; likewise if the hammer doesn't have sufficient weight, you will have to use more force than is necessary.

SANDPAPER All frames will need sanding to smooth joints, or in preparation for paint or stain. Use a fine grade sandpaper available from any hardware or DIY store.

MITRE CLAMP This will ensure you can glue and nail your components into a true right angle. It holds the wood by clamping it tightly together. Some clamps have an extension so that you can put right-angled moulding pins in from the back of the frame. This is recommended if you are doing a lot of framing. This will only be available from framing specialists (see Suppliers List, page 94). A simple mitre clamp should also be available from carpenters' suppliers.

FRAME CLAMP This will hold your frame at true right angles while the glue dries. It is not very expensive to buy from a specialist supplier, but you can make your own from four solid 45 degree angles and a piece of string.

D RINGS These are used with screws or split pins to hang the picture on the wall. The advantage is that they keep the frame fairly flat against the wall. They are available through some glass merchants or through framing catalogues and stockists (see page 94).

SCREW EYES You may prefer to use these as an alternative to D rings, but they will hold the frame slightly away from the wall.

CORD OR WIRE I prefer using nylon cord to traditional picture wire. However, a very heavy picture will require wire. Nylon cord is available from DIY stores, picture framers and haberdashery departments.

MITRE SAW If you plan to make a lot of frames, a mitre saw is an easier way of cutting to an angle. It will also allow you to make hexagonal shapes as you can choose the angle you want to cut. A mitre saw is available from DIY stores or tool stockists but is generally expensive and, if you are inexperienced at using one, it will take some practice to develop the skill to operate it.

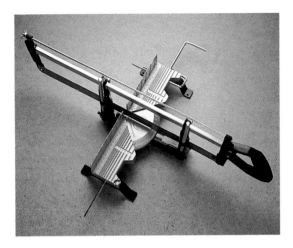

If you're planning to tackle a lot of framing, you might want to invest in a mitre saw. It is a more sophisticated version of a mitre block and hand saw, but is more accurate and reliable.

. . . .

MOUNTING

Mounting materials must – above all – be clean and straight-edged, and the blade in your knife must be sharp. The better the conditions of your tools, the more professional the result.

MOUNT BOARD There are many colours of mount board available: from white to black, marbled to mottled. Keep the board stored in a clean, dry place and preferably flat rather than standing on its edge. It is available in both A1 and A2 sheets and most suppliers should let you have a sample book which you can keep at home for reference.

Coloured mount board is basically a white board with decorative paper adhered to both sides, so no matter what colour you buy, the edge will show white when you cut it.

Mount board is available from art suppliers, but framing specialists will stock a larger range.

CUTTING MAT This is an essential part of mounting, providing a safe and clean surface on which to cut your board. The mat is a self-healing rubber which allows you to put pressure on your knife without damaging the blade.

Ensure you have plenty of space around the mat as a cramped space creates wobbly cutting. Most art and craft suppliers will stock cutting mats.

T SQUARE A T square with a rubberized backing is very useful for cutting. It does not slip and will ensure you cut at a right angle.

CUTTING KNIFE Choose a strong steel craft knife.

MOUNT CUTTER A small, hand-held mount cutter is quite inexpensive and easy to use. Most art and craft suppliers will be able to obtain one for you, even if they do not have one in stock. Buy extra blades so that the one you use is always razor sharp.

The larger mount cutter shown on page 21 is still only a piece of hobby equipment and not a professional item, so it is not extremely expensive. It is very easy to operate and will guarantee a straight and accurate line every time. It is a good investment if you are planning lots of framing and mounting.

TAPE There are a variety of tapes on the market, but brown paper tape is the most useful to the framer. Use it to stick artwork on to a background. Because the tape is made of paper it will react to ambient conditions in the same way as the artwork itself, so you will avoid any creasing or buckling. A ready-gummed brown tape is good for sealing the back of the frame as it will prevent dampness from entering and mouldering the mount and picture inside.

Although masking tape is handy, it is best only used for temporary positioning, as the brown tapes are longer-lasting and superior.

SCISSORS Only use scissors for tape or paper. Do not attempt to cut board with them as you will never achieve a completely straight and true line.

OTHER ITEMS A clean, clear **ruler** is useful for measuring and drawing lines. Use an **H pencil** with a sharp point for accurate line drawing. Keep an **artist's soft eraser** to hand for removing dirty finger marks or erasing mistakes.

HAND DRILL

TENON SAW

MITRE CLAMP

T SQUARE

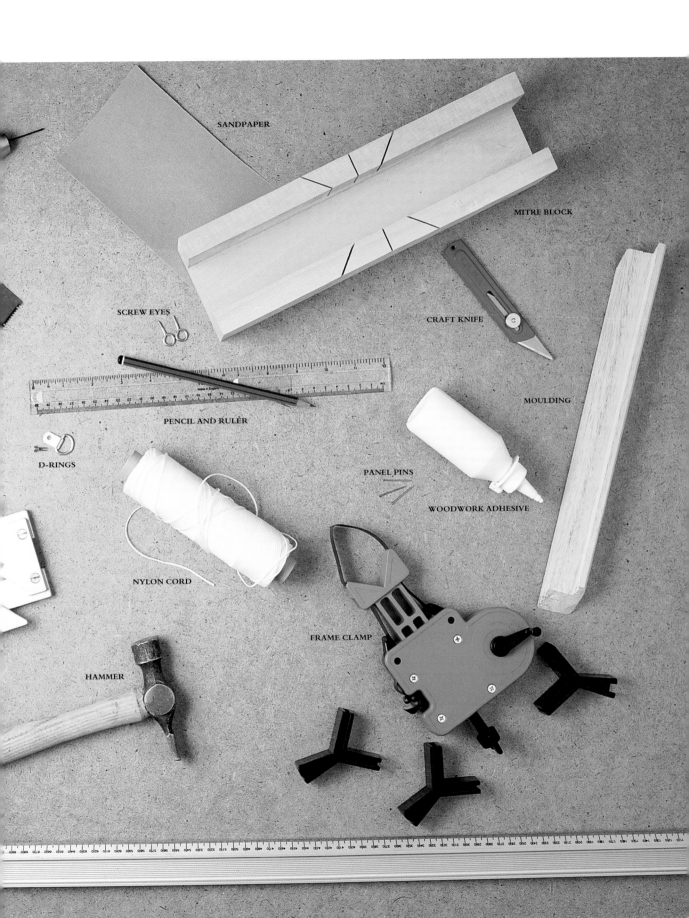

SANDPAPER

MITRE BLOCK

SCREW EYES

CRAFT KNIFE

MOULDING

PENCIL AND RULER

D-RINGS

PANEL PINS

WOODWORK ADHESIVE

NYLON CORD

FRAME CLAMP

HAMMER

STAINS, PAINTS AND WOOD FINISHES

There are many different ways to finish your frame. If you have the opportunity, experiment with a range of finishes to decide which effects you like best.

STAINS These are either water- or spirit-based. Unlike paint, which can completely cover the surface, stains allow the texture and grain of the wood to show through. Most people are familiar with wood stains which are readily available from DIY outlets. These enable you to transform a pale softwood into a rich mahogany, dark oak or other wood of your choice.

Also available are coloured stains. Although the water-based stains may have a tendency to fade, they are more pleasant to use as they have little odour. They are available ready-mixed or in powder form from most timber suppliers or specialists. Spirit-based colours come in a wide range of long-lasting shades.

PAINTS Emulsion paints are really useful, especially if you experiment with small testers which cost so little. To create a wash rather than a solid, covering colour, simply water down the paint.

Acrylic paint is available in pots or tubes from art shops. Although it is fairly expensive to buy, it comes in a wide range of colours and it can also be used to tint emulsion paint. It can give a solid finish or a wash.

The other paint used for framing is gold gilding paint which is a spirit-based lacquer. This is easy to apply especially over a red or black painted base which shows as an antique warmth through the gold.

BRUSHES It is worth investing in good quality brushes. Cheap brushes will simply shed hairs and give an uneven finish. A long-handled brush with a flat head will make painting easier. Use an artist's fine brush for detail.

GESSO This is a chalky powder which when

MOUNT BOARD

MASKING TAPE

CRAFT KNIFE

BROWN PAPER TAPE

PENCIL, RULER AND ERASER

COMPASS

CUTTING MAT

HAND-HELD
MOUNT CUTTER

T SQUARE

WAX POLISH

GOLD PAINT

SANDPAPER

BLACK PAINT

PAINTBRUSHES

READY-MIXED GESSO

POLYURETHANE AND ACRYLIC VARNISH

WOOD STAIN

WHITE SPIRIT

ACRYLIC PAINTS

SOFT CLOTH

mixed with size is used to create a smooth and absorbent surface to a frame in preparation for gold leaf or other paint techniques. It also comes in a ready-made paste which is quicker to use (see pages 17 and 89 for more details on gesso.)

VARNISH Acrylic varnish is sufficient for most frames, although you can use polyurethane if you have some to hand. Available in matt, satin or high gloss, varnish will protect the paint or wood finish. Varnish is also available in a spray

can which is useful on awkward shapes. Acrylic varnish is sold by hardware stores or DIY outlets.

WAX For a natural finish on unpainted wood, apply a layer of furniture wax with a soft cloth. This can then be buffed up to a wonderful lustre which will enhance the wood.

WHITE SPIRIT OR METHYLATED SPIRITS White spirit is used to clean oil-based paints, methylated spirits will clean spirit-based stains.

GOLD SIZE

WHITING

GOLD LEAF BRUSH

IMITATION GOLD LEAF

SIZE GRANULES

GILDING

A traditional technique used to decorate plaster or wooden frames to give an ornate gold finish. This quite skilful technique is still in use today and although gold leaf is quite expensive, imitation gold leaf gives almost as good a result. All these products are available from specialist outlets or mail order (see Suppliers, page 94).

FINE WHITING POWDER This is basically a white chalky powder used for making **gesso**. The white paste is applied in layers to the frame and sanded down to create a smooth, absorbent surface (see page 89).

SIZE GRANULES An ancient gilding material, these granules are sometimes referred to as rabbit glue because they are made from the skin and other by-products of these animals. It is mixed with whiting to make gesso.

GOLD LEAF Pure gold leaf is a beautiful colour and will not need varnishing. It is, however, quite expensive. Imitation gold leaf, on the other hand, is less expensive but as it is quite a crude colour and it tarnishes, it will need to be varnished with white polish or shellac.

Silver and bronze leaf are also available.

Imitation gold leaf comes in a loose leaf form, which is good for multifaceted surfaces. It also comes with a tissue paper backing which is easier to use on flat surfaces.

GOLD SIZE This is a clear honey-coloured glue designed for sticking gold leaf on to a surface prepared with gesso.

GOLD LEAF BRUSH As you should not touch gold leaf – it is very fragile and will puncture – this very delicate brush makes handling the leaf much easier.

SHELLAC OR WHITE POLISH These are solvent-based substances which are used for protecting the surface of frames gilded with imitation gold leaf. Shellac is a honey-coloured varnish which will slightly dull the colour of the gold; white polish is clear and will not change the colour of the item but simply act as a protective sealant.

BASIC TECHNIQUES

If you enjoy DIY or woodwork, this section will present you with little difficulty. If, on the other hand, you are an absolute beginner, do not be daunted as these fundamental skills are perfected with practice. You need only the most basic tools — just remember to keep knives and blades sharp, let the saw — not your arm — do the work. It is worth bearing in mind that any carpentry work will be messy, and should be carried out well away from any mounting, which must be kept as clean as possible.

MAKING A FRAME

Begin by preparing the mitre block. You might find it easier to screw it on to your work surface to prevent it from moving about. Place a piece of 5 x 2.5 cm (2 x 1 in) wood inside to lift up the floor of the block. Place one end of your

These simple picture frames are all made to a similar square shape, yet they each look quite different depending on the choice of moulding used.

. . . .

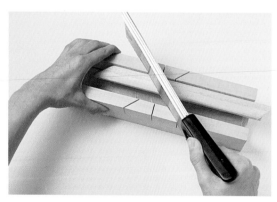

Cut the moulding at a true right angle with a mitre block and tenon saw.

. . . .

wood or moulding in the mitre block, hold it firmly against the inside edge and cut it to an angle of 45 degrees with a tenon saw.

Measure along the length from the outer edge of the corner you have just cut and mark with a pencil. Place the wood back in the block and cut it at the opposite 45 degree angle inwards from your mark. Repeat this on the other three pieces of moulding until you have four pieces the correct size.

At this point, check your frame sits neatly together. If not, trim off a little all round.

With the moulding secure in the mitre clamp, moulding pins are hammered in at an angle to hold the pieces together.

. . . .

Place two edges into the mitre clamp, put a little wood adhesive into the join and clamp the pieces together. Using strong pliers, take the head off a moulding pin and use this instead of a drill bit in a hand drill. Drill a hole at an angle joining the two pieces together. Hammer in another moulding pin. Repeat this on the other three corners.

A frame clamp ensures a sturdy and secure frame.

. . . .

At this stage, you can check your corners are square and leave the frame to dry overnight. However, to be sure the frame is accurate and true, use a frame clamp. Place the frame inside the clamp and tighten the angles around it. Leave it in this position until it is dry.

If there are any open joints, you can fill them quite neatly and quickly with fine sawdust and a little wood adhesive. When dry, the joints can be sanded smooth.

STAINING

There are a variety of stains available (see page 14). For the best finish, use a cloth to apply the wood stain. You can build up the colour by applying further coats, leaving each one to dry

A lightly stained frame is buffed to a lustrous finish with some furniture wax and a soft cloth.

. . . .

before adding the next. When the frame is completely dry, apply a little wax to the surface. Let the wax soak into the wood before buffing it with a soft cloth. Another coat of wax will add even more lustre.

MOUNTING AND FIXING

Instead of simply framing your piece of art, mounting it with special board can enhance it tremendously if time is taken to do it well. Mount board is available in a wide selection of colours, but a simple cream or white mount will often be the answer. It is also possible to double mount. This is to place a darker colour down first then a larger, lighter colour on top to create an inner frame.

The most important aspect of successful mounting is to use clean, sharp equipment. Any fingermarks, grease or rough edges will be quickly noticed. Give yourself plenty of space and time and ensure all your cutting tools have sharp blades.

Select a mount to complement your picture and decide what area of the picture you would like to see. It is usual to mount a picture with an equal amount of border all around, perhaps giving the lower border a little more width.

Turn the frame over and measure the inside – edge to edge. Using the cutting mat, set square

Use a pencil and ruler to measure the mount board.
. . . .

and knife, cut out a piece of board the same size as the inside of the frame.

With the good side facing down, decide how large you want the window to be. Take the

A hand-held mount cutter will give an accurate bevelled edge to the board, creating a professional finish.
. . . .

window measurement away from the frame measurement and divide the remainder in two. This is the distance from the side. Draw out the rectangle and raise the lower line by a few millimetres (fractions of an inch) if you wish.

Here, a small mount cutter is used; this will cut the edges of the window at a 45 degree angle. Cut out the shape from the back; be cautious at the corners and if you are unsure, practise on some scrap board first.

Measure the back of the frame and have a piece of glass cut to fit (you can do this yourself if you use a glass cutter and straight edge). You will also need to saw a piece of hardboard to the same size. Both pieces should fit easily into the back of the frame. Drill small holes into the back of the hardboard to accommodate the D rings. (You may prefer to screw the D rings into the

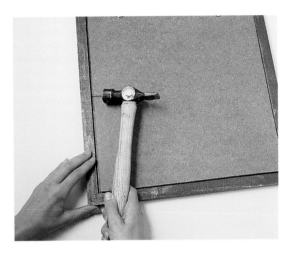

To secure the backing to the frame, nail small panel pins into the sides.

. . . .

the frame and with a hammer, nail small panel pins into the sides of the frame to secure it. Stick tape around the back of the frame to prevent dust, damp or insects creeping in and spoiling

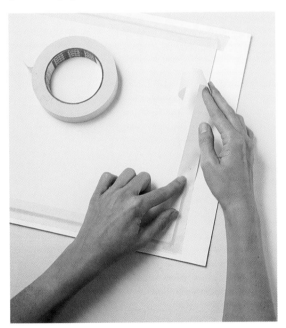

Masking tape is useful to position the picture on the mount board. For long-term fixing, use brown paper tape.

. . . .

back verticals of the frame itself.)

Using brown paper gummed tape, stick the print down on the back of the mount, checking your image is straight. Place all the pieces into

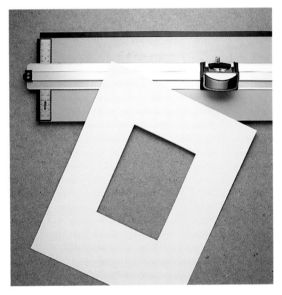

For large amounts of mounting, a flat mount cutter may be a worthwhile investment. This device is quick and easy to operate, although it does cost more than the hand-held cutter shown opposite.

. . . .

GALLERY

ON THE FOLLOWING PAGES, we showcase work from contemporary designers who specialize in frames. The various works on display represent a wide range of media, including wood, metal, glass and fabric, and each one demonstrates a variety of techniques and skills to achieve the finished piece.

Although some of the frames featured cover techniques which are beyond the scope of this book, I hope you will browse, absorb and find inspiration from the pieces shown here to adapt and originate your own ideas.

~

Nautical Frames
SHOELESS JOE
This selection of seashore-inspired frames are fashioned principally from hand-painted wood and pieces of chunky rope. These frames demonstrate just how successful the most simple ideas can be: witness the wide, box type frame holding the little wooden carved boat.

Mirrored Mosaic

REBECCA NEWNHAM
Rebecca Newnham specializes in two and three dimensional mosaics for commission and a limited range of mirrors which are sold around the world. This circular mirrored mosaic framed mirror is 100 cm (40 in) in diameter.

Alphabet Frame

ANNE TAYLOR
A very simple wooden frame has been transformed by a combination of detailed hand painting and stencilling to produce a charming addition to the nursery or child's bedroom.

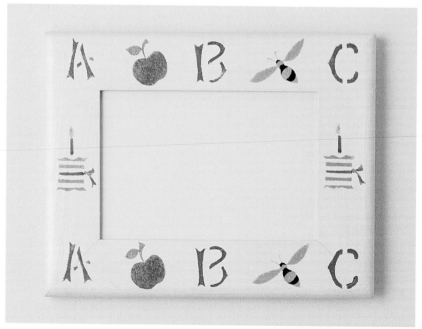

Metal Fish Mirror

PAUL NORTHERNER

Inspired by travel to Indonesia, this fishy themed mirror uses cut and 'blued' metal, twisted and welded together to create the underwater scene.

Papier Mâché and Embroidery Frame

CLAIRE SOWDEN

A fabulous contemporary frame constructed from papier mâché and intricate machine embroidery. Claire's main influences come from Islamic and Indian artefacts and architecture – imagery which she finds magical in terms of shape, texture and colour.

Equestrian Mirror

BARBARA DIZDAR

This ornate mirror with its lavish theatrical style and heavy ornamentation was inspired by visits to many ancient sites and museums. Here, the mirror is treated as a landscape depicting an ancient, crumbling Greek ruin.

Celtic Shield Mirror

WILDE AT ART

This classic circular frame has a Celtic braided detail taken from the Battersea shield. It is given an antique appearance by the silver gilding process.

Egyptian Mirror

WILDE AT ART

The artists at Wilde at Art specialize in gilding techniques and this Egyptian-inspired mirror is an excellent example of the art. To create a sense of authenticity, the gold leaf is carefully rubbed back to reveal the red and black 'bole' beneath. The cornice at the top reflects the style of early Egyptian architecture.

Jester Mirror
SUZANNE MALYON

This bold, contemporary shape is made from wood and plaster, then decorated with gold leaf and paints. As an established painter and artist, Suzanne enjoys experimenting with colours best of all, and employs various techniques to achieve some exciting paint effects on her frames.

Bashed Metal Mirror
SASHA BOWLES

Beating a design on to the reverse of sheet pewter was a technique widely used in the art nouveau period at the turn of the century, and one which is now being rediscovered. Contrary to the common perception of metal, Sasha finds this material tactile and sensuous and perfect for framing.

Musical Collage
BARBARA DIZDAR
This mirror incorporates a musical collage of trumpets and violins mixed with shield and sword imagery.

Heraldic Frame
ANNE TAYLOR
Traditional images such as the fleur-de-lys (below left) never really lose their style. This elegant picture frame has been painted and stencilled in complementary colours to achieve this classical finish.

Embroidered Frames
CLAIRE SOWDEN
These tiny embroidered mirror frames have been worked in a variety of silks using appliqué and heavy stitch work to create an intensity of colour and rich texture. The padding gives each one a most distinctive character.

TIN FISH FRAME

BARBARA DIZDAR

THIS FISHY FRAME is made from recycled wood to create a worn, sea-washed look. Thin washes of paint allow the grain to show through, and the simple tin fish provide a bold contrast in texture.

This frame allows you to use old rough, weathered wood from a variety of sources. Driftwood from the sea is lovely, but this frame uses rather battered wood taken from a builder's disused palette.

~

MATERIALS AND EQUIPMENT

- *6mm (¼ in) plywood or MDF* • *old planks of wood from palette or similar* • *saw* • *drill* • *jigsaw* • *sandpaper* • *wood adhesive* • *carpet tacks* • *panel pins* • *white emulsion paint* • *paintbrush* • *blue acrylic paint* • *old tin cans* • *old pair of scissors* • *wire wool* • *screwdriver* • *hammer* • *black felt tip pen*
  . . . . . .

1 Decide on the size of your frame and cut the plywood into a rectangle, 1 cm (¾ in) smaller all round. Gauge the width of the frame by laying one plank of recycled wood in position and marking it. Do this on all sides to give the inner rectangle. Use the jigsaw to cut out the centre section. The recycled wood must overhang the plywood base by at least 1 cm (⅜ in) all round. Cut the recycled wood to size. Trickle on wood glue and stick down each piece. Secure the wood with carpet tacks. Turn the frame over and secure with panel pins or screws.

2 Mix up some white emulsion paint with water, in a 1:10 ratio. Paint over the whole frame with this white 'wash' and leave to dry thoroughly.

3 Now mix a watery blue wash using acrylic paint and water. Apply this to the frame and leave to dry thoroughly.

4 Wash the old tin cans well and open them up flat. Cut out fish shapes and fish tails (following the photograph here) using an old pair of scissors. Take care, as the edges can be very sharp. Rub the edges with wire wool to dull the sharpness. Turn the fish shapes on to their backs and, using a screwdriver and hammer, knock small indentations into the fish to represent scales, gills, etc.

5 Secure the fish on to the frame by nailing one tack through the eye and one through the double tail. Highlight the eye with a black felt-tip pen. Mount the glass or picture in the frame as described on pages 20-21.

TRIPTYCH

BARBARA DIZDAR

THIS IS ONE OF THE OLDEST, most mystical of shapes. Originally designed to carry religious icons or relics from place to place, the doors folded inwards to protect the pictures on journeys and pilgrimages. This mirror derives its inspiration from those magnificent gold icon paintings, but is cruder, more Gothic and somewhat reminiscent of a small village church.

~

MATERIALS AND EQUIPMENT

- *60 x 60 cm x 12 mm (2 x 2 ft x ½ in) MDF*
- *1 x 1 m x 6 mm (3 x 3 ft x ¼ in) MDF* • *3 mirrors cut to size of patterns B and E (see page 92)* • *small candleholder* • *4 small hinges*
- *15 coloured glass stones*
- *brown emulsion paint*
- *gold and green acrylic paint*
- *16 x 12 mm (½ in) screws*
- *wood adhesive* • *contact adhesive* • *all-purpose glue*
- *satin varnish* • *white spirit*
- *2 'D' rings* • *sandpaper*
- *drill* • *jigsaw* • *chisel*
- *2.5 cm (1 in) paintbrush*
- *detailing paintbrush*
- *screwdriver*
. . . . . .

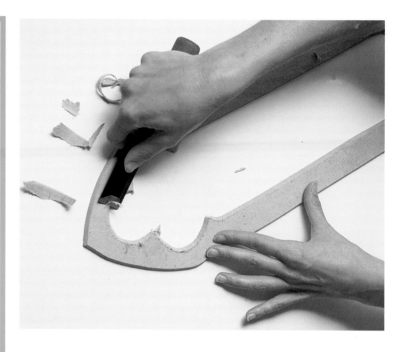

1 Using the patterns on page 92, mark out one piece A and two pieces D on the thicker MDF. Cut out the three pieces with a jigsaw, angling the edges at roughly 45 degrees. On the thinner MDF, mark out patterns B and C. Cut these two pieces out. Now mark out patterns E and F twice on to the thinner MDF to give you four more pieces. Once again chamfer the edges. Once you have assembled the nine pieces, chisel the edges (always away from you) to give a hand-carved appearance. Take care at this stage not to chisel away too much, and pay special attention to the curved edges.

2 Sand all the surfaces on each piece with medium grade sandpaper. Although this is a rather tedious task, it will ensure a good finish later.

3 Drill five holes in piece C and both F pieces as shown to create small recesses for the glass stones. Chisel around the recesses, but make sure they are smaller than the stones. Sand the newly carved edges.

4 Place the candleholder on a scrap of the 12 mm (½ in) MDF and draw around it with a pencil. To complete the shape, you will need to inscribe a small curve either side of the circle you have drawn. Use the candleholder as shown to give you this shape. Make sure the curved pieces either side of the circle extend at least 1.5 cm (⅝ in). Carefully cut this piece out with the jigsaw.

5 Chisel the candle shelf in the same way as the other pieces and sand it down. Drill two holes at the outer ends ready for the screws. As the screws should be countersunk, use a special drill bit, or chisel the holes to allow for this.

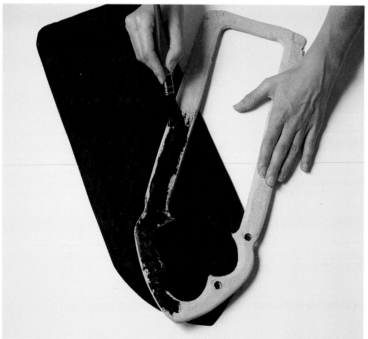

6 Prime all the components with brown emulsion paint, including the candle shelf. When dry, paint all the pieces with a coat of the green paint.

7 Mix gold acrylic with a little
dark green and add a little
water. Paint the edges of all the
pieces with this watery gold,
highlighting the top of the arch
on pieces C and F with a brighter
gold. Use the detailing brush and
gold acrylic to paint a few tiny
leaves or floral devices for
decoration, as you wish. Leave to
dry thoroughly.

8 Using the wood adhesive,
stick pieces A and B together.
Stick together one D piece and
one E piece. Repeat with the
remaining D and E pieces.
Varnish all the pieces.

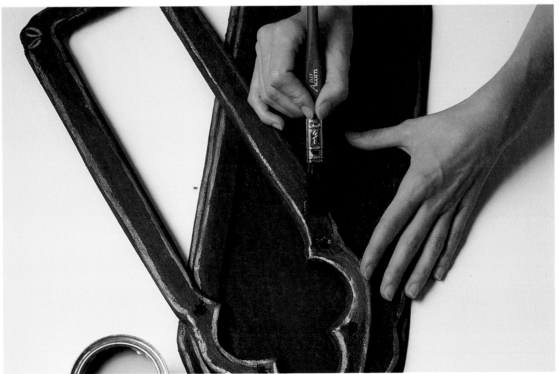

9 Take the three pre-cut mirrors and glue inside B and the two E pieces using contact adhesive. Weight them down and leave to dry. Working from the back make small holes at the top and two sides of the frames, taking care not to drill all the way through and avoiding the mirror. Screw each frame together.

10 Stick the coloured glass stones into the prepared holes with all-purpose glue.

11 Using wood adhesive, glue the candleshelf into position on the central piece. Finally, screw the shelf through the pre-drilled holes on to the frame.

12 Turn the frame over and screw the hinges in place. Screw on the D rings and tie a cord to the back.

CHECKERED FRAME

LYNETTE WRIGLEY

DECORATING A SIMPLE FRAME with squares of opalescent glass takes minutes, yet the result is classic. It is not expensive to buy the glass and it is quite straightforward to cut using a carbide glass cutter. If you are not confident handling glass, give the measurements to a stained glass supplier (see page 94) who will be happy to cut the pieces for you.

Although black and cream glass have been used here, you could use different colours. Good glass stockists will have a wide range to choose from.

~

MATERIALS AND EQUIPMENT

● *simple frame* ● *20 x 20 cm (8 x 8 in) black opalescent glass* ● *20 x 20 cm (8 x 8 in) cream opalescent glass* ● *ruler* ● *felt tip pen* ● *carbide glass cutter (optional) straight edge (optional)* ● *wet and dry sandpaper* ● *all-purpose clear adhesive*
. . . . . .

1 Using a ruler, divide each side of the frame into equal sections. Measure both the width and the length of each side. This will give you the dimensions for the glass squares.

2 Transfer the measurements on to the glass using a ruler and felt tip pen. Remember that half the squares will be from black glass and half from cream glass. Either take the marked pieces of glass to the supplier to be cut, or cut them yourself using a glass cutter and straight edge.

3 Polish the edges of the glass squares with wet and dry sandpaper. This is essential for a neat and safe finish.

4 Lay the squares on to the frame, checking they all fit accurately. (You might need to switch them about to get a really good fit.) Apply adhesive to the back of each square and stick them down.

DISPLAY BOX

BARBARA DIZDAR

ALMOST EVERYONE COLLECTS little objects which are principally of sentimental value. Rather than keeping them hidden at the back of a drawer or in a trinket box, make this antique-style display box to 'frame' these small family heirlooms.

The frame requires some fundamental woodwork skills, but only a few basic tools. It is decorated with photocopied enlargements of old family snapshots, pictures and drawings, which personalises this project even more, making it very much your own special treasure trove.

~

MATERIALS AND EQUIPMENT

- *4 m x 6-8 cm x 2 cm (6 ft x 2-3 in x ¼ in) softwood*
- *scrap of 6 mm (¼ in) MDF or plywood at least 50 cm (20 in) square* • *photocopies*
- *2.5 cm (1 in) screws*
- *2.5 cm (1 in) panel pins*
- *wood adhesive* • *PVA glue*
- *yellow/cream-coloured emulsion paint* • *white matt spray paint* • *ruler*
- *screwdriver* • *drill* • *hand saw* • *chisel* • *hammer*
. . . . . .

1 Cut the wood into 6 x 42 cm (16 ¾ in) lengths. Measure in exactly 11 cm (4 ½ in) from the end of one piece, mark this with a pencil, then measure in 11 cm (4 ½ in) from the other end of the same piece and mark this too. Now draw a line 1 cm (⅜ in) either side of the first mark, to give you a 2 cm (¾ in) area which you will later cut out. Repeat this on the other mark, then again on three other pieces of wood. This will give you four pieces, each with two notches marked. Cut into the notches with a hand saw, sawing about halfway down the wood. Use a chisel to finish cutting out.

2 Slot the four pieces of wood together to form a grid.

3 Cut a further two lengths of wood, this time measuring 46 cm (18 ½ in). Take these and the two remaining 42 cm (16 ¾ in) lengths of wood and screw them around the outside of the grid to form the outer walls of the box.

4 Take the MDF or plywood and check that at least two of the corners are a true right angle. Align these corners with two corners of the frame and nail into place, using a few panel pins.

5 Saw off the other two sides of the backing which are now overhanging. Putting the backing on to the frame in this way will give you a perfect fit.

6 Take the various photocopies and work out how you want to arrange them in the box. Remember that you will need to cover all the edges and sides, so it is worth hunting round for suitable border designs to trim the edges. Cut the photocopies to fit and glue them down with the diluted PVA adhesive.

7 When the photocopies are in place and dry, cover the box with a thin wash of watery yellow paint to blend all the pictures together and give them an aged, mellowed look.

8 Spray the background of each niche with a little white spray paint, to help your chosen objects stand out against the busy background.

HARVEST MICE

MOIRA NEAL

FOR THOSE UNFAMILIAR with doughcraft, this novel frame with its tiny mice scampering across the plaited wheat, is made from salt dough. Salt dough is very easy to make from store cupboard ingredients. It is baked in a domestic oven and then varnished to protect it from damp.

This heart-shape design is simple to adapt to an oval or circular mirror. For a heart-shaped mirror have the mirror cut at the glass store, using the pattern on page 93. Seal the mirror to the frame with silicone.

~

MATERIALS AND EQUIPMENT

- *2 level cups of plain flour*
- *1 level cup of salt* • *¾ cup of water* • *instant coffee powder* • *piece of wire*
- *peppercorns* • *varnish*
- *mixing bowl* • *cling film*
- *knife* • *small pointed scissors* • *baking tray*
- *paintbrush* • *old pencil*
. . . . . .

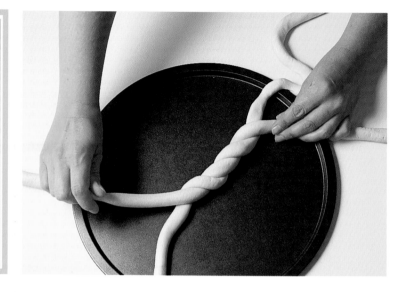

1 Mix the dry ingredients and then add the water. Mix to a dough, then turn on to a work surface and knead thoroughly for 10 minutes. The dough should be firm but slightly tacky. If necessary, add a little more water. Keep the dough covered with cling film until you are ready to use it. Take three-quarters of dough and divide into two. Enlarge the pattern on page 93, and use this as a guide for the size of the frame. Roll each piece into a long rope at least one-third longer than the outside edge of the template. Working from the centre, take the right hand rope and lay it over the middle one; take the left hand rope and lay this over the middle one. Continue in this way until the twisted rope is long enough to 'frame' the template. Join the ends with a little water.

2 Form the rope into a heart shape, using the template as a guide. Join the shape at the top and pinch the dough together to secure it. This join will be covered later by the ears of wheat. Carefully, insert a loop of stiff wire into the back at the top to enable the frame to be hung.

3 To make the ears of wheat, make small sausage shapes from some of the remaining dough. Take the sharp-pointed scissors and snip into the dough at an angle to create the texture of the wheat.

4 Roll out some thin sausage shapes to resemble the stalks of wheat, bunch these together and trim with the scissors. Using a little water, stick these into place at the top of the heart then add the ears of wheat.

5 To make the mice, mix a tablespoon of instant coffee with some boiling water to form a thick liquid paste. When cool, knead this into the remaining dough. For the mice bodies, roll the dough into small oval-shaped balls. Push the point of the old pencil into the head to allow for the ears, and lower down for the eyes. Moisten two peppercorns and set these into the eye sockets. The ears are small circles of dough which are pinched at one end and pushed into the holes you have just made. Dampen them first so that they stick. For the tails, roll out thin sausage shapes. Push a pencil hole into the base of the mouse, dampen the tail and stick it in place. For those mice with paws, use small pieces of dough, marking them to resemble claws. Follow the main photograph for the positions of the mice.

6 Bake immediately in a fan-assisted oven at 80°C or conventional oven at 100°C for about 8-12 hours or until the dough is rock solid. For a gas oven bake on mark ¼ for 1 hour with the door open, then a further hour with the door half-closed, and the last 2-6 hours with the door shut. Varnish when cool. (Although unlikely, this frame could in time become damp, which could loosen its fixing. It is therefore safer not to hang in a children's room or above the bed.)

BAROQUE MIRROR

BARBARA DIZDAR

THIS FRAME PROVIDES a great contradiction. We know the material is cardboard, yet the overall effect is directly inspired by the splendour of the former kings and queens of France. A good example of recycling, it looks quite magnificent. It is also easy to make, requiring few tools or materials.

〜

MATERIALS AND EQUIPMENT

• *2 very large 4-ply cardboard boxes* • *1.5 m x 60 cm (5 ft x 2 ft) corrugated cardboard* • *white emulsion paint* • *mirror cut to fit circle of pattern B* • *2 'D' rings and fittings* • *contact adhesive* • *glue gun* • *scissors* • *5 cm (2 in) paintbrush*
......

1 Flatten out the large cardboard boxes. Enlarge the patterns on page 93 and transfer on to the flattened cardboard. Cut out the shapes using scissors, but do not worry if the cardboard tears slightly, as all the edges will be covered later. Using the glue gun, stick piece B on top of piece D, aligning the feet only.

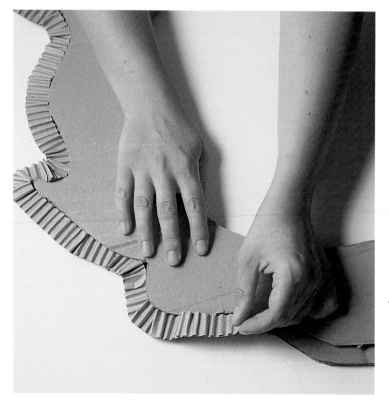

2 Turn the frame over. Cut the corrugated cardboard into 2 cm (¾ in) strips. Keep the strips as long as possible to avoid ugly joins. Begin to glue a strip around the edge of the frame, leaving the base of the feet bare. Concertina and fan out the corrugated strips to fit neatly around the curves. (The corrugated cardboard is very malleable and easy to work with.)

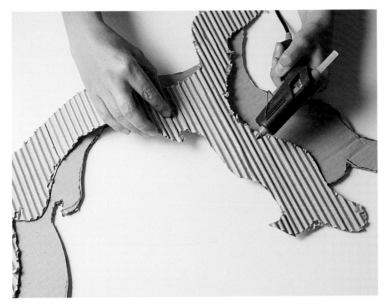

3 Cut out another section C, but this time in corrugated cardboard, and glue it on top of the first piece. Stick this complete piece centrally on to the frame, keeping the feet level.

4 Using more thin corrugated strips, cover all the edges of C. Cut out some 1 cm (⅜ in) strips of corrugated cardboard and glue these over the outer edge of D. Use more 1 cm (⅜ in) strips to create a second layer of decoration around the edge of C. Continue this strip vertically around the inside edge of the frame, where the mirror will sit.

5 Glue a 2.5 cm (1 in) strip of corrugated cardboard around the top inside edge of the circle. All the original cardboard edges should now be covered in corrugated strips, except the base of the feet.

6 To create the fan at the top of the frame, cut a piece of corrugated cardboard measuring 35 x 10 cm (14 x 4 in). Concertina the piece together, then fan it out at the top as shown. Glue this in position.

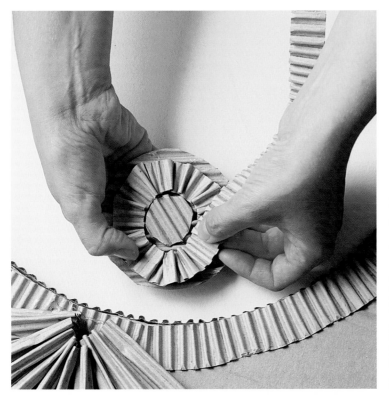

7 For the rosette, cut a 7 cm (2 ¾ in) circle and a 3 cm (1 ¼ in) circle from corrugated cardboard. Glue the smaller piece on top of the larger circle. Now cut a 2 cm (¾ in) strip of corrugated cardboard and ruffle this all around the outer circle. Glue into place. Stick the completed rosette on the bottom of the fan.

8 To make the curlicues on either side of the fan and at the base, cut three 2 cm (¾ in) strips. Curl one into a small circle next to the fan. Glue the remainder of the strip into position, and finish with another small circle. Repeat this for the other two curlicues.

9 To make the bow, cut a strip of corrugated cardboard measuring 22 x 20 cm (8 ¾ x 8 in), squeeze it in the middle and secure it with a small strip of cardboard. Cut two small strips to serve as 'tails' and glue them on to the back of the bow. Stick the bow to the base of the frame.

10 Cut a 1 cm (⅜ in) strip of corrugated cardboard, curl one end and gently flatten this small circle, as shown. Glue in place. Take the remainder of the strip and pull it up on to its side, so that the raw edge faces you. Glue this into place, finishing with a final curl. Repeat this step three more times, following the photograph of the finished frame.

11 Cut two pieces of corrugated cardboard 2.5 x 18 cm (1 x 7 in), concertina them into two small fans and glue on to the top of the feet. Paint the whole frame, including section A with cream-coloured emulsion.

12 Attach 'D' rings to section A. Turn the frame over, smear glue over the recess and stick the mirror into place. Using the contact adhesive, glue section A firmly down on to the rest of the frame to hold the mirror in place.

SEASHELL DECOUPAGE

BARBARA DIZDAR

THIS SIMPLE BUT STYLISH frame illustrates the use of decoupage: the French term that describes the decoration of surfaces with paper cut-outs. In this project, the technique is used on a round, wooden frame which is straightforward to make from MDF. The central compartment is ideal for housing a collage of small objects. Here, a collection of shells echoes the pictures decorating the surrounding frame.

When selecting suitable images for decoupage, choose a paper without a reverse side: wrapping paper or photocopies are good options.

~

1 Using a compass, draw a circle with a diameter of 35 cm (14 in) on to a piece of 12 cm (½ in) thick MDF. Cut out the circle with a jigsaw. Place the point of the compass on the central point and draw another circle – 18 cm (7 in) in diameter. This forms the basic frame.

2 To make the backing, place a piece of 6 mm (¼ in) thick board under the frame and inscribe round the inner circle with a pencil, marking several notches on both the backing board and the inside of the circle. Once cut out, these notches can be used to align with each other to give you an accurate guide when slotting the pieces together.

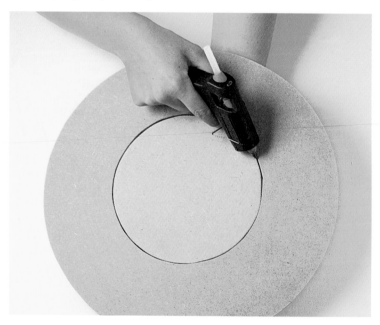

3 Working from the back, glue the thinner backing board inside the inner circle of the basic frame, marrying the notches and using a glue gun. Turn the frame over to the front and smooth over the join with filler. When the filler is dry, paint the whole frame with one coat of cream emulsion paint.

4 Once the first coat of paint is dry, coat the frame again, this time with a mixture of cream and blue emulsion. For the best effect, don't mix the paints, but brush them on at the same time so that they merge to create a sea-like wash. Leave to dry.

5 Cut out the paper images with a pair of sharp scissors and arrange them around the frame. When you are happy with the position of the images, stick them in place with PVA adhesive. Apply a coat of PVA over the frame to protect the paint and secure the images.

TROMPE L'OEIL

TABBY RILEY

THIS CLEVER EFFECT, meaning 'trick of the eye', is a traditional paint technique which is amazingly simple to do. It is the positioning of the tones of colour that creates this striking three-dimensional effect.

The use of the soft, earthy colours and the addition of a slightly textured surface gives the frame the appearance of Italian fresco. Although you can alter the choice of colours, remember that the success of this technique is the close harmony of tones. Those used here are beige, dark apricot, light apricot and cream.

~

MATERIALS AND EQUIPMENT

● *wooden frame* ● *interior plaster filler* ● *plasterer's float* ● *pencil* ● *ruler* ● *set square* ● *acrylic or emulsion paint in four toning colours* ● *matt acrylic varnish* ● *paintbrush* ● *small natural sponge*
. . . . . .

1 Spread the filler on to the frame in a fairly random way using the plasterer's float. Aim for an uneven, patchy finish. Leave to dry.

2 Using a ruler and set square, divide the edge of the frame into squares, as shown. Mark lightly with pencil.

3 Divide each square into four triangles, drawing the lines in fine pencil.

4 Thin the first colour with a little water. Using the brush, paint on to one triangle of the first square. Repeat this on each of the subsequent squares, making sure you paint the same triangle in each square.

5 Before the first colour has dried, thin the second colour and apply in the same way. Take care to keep the paint within the lines you have drawn.

6 Now use the third colour. Dab a sponge on to the wet colours, to help break up the surface slightly and create a softer look, but be careful not to merge the colours into each other.

7 Finish with the fourth colour,
dabbing the surface as in step
6 to soften it.

8 Leave the paint to dry
thoroughly, then finish with a
coat of varnish for protection.

LACE AND FLOWERS

BARBARA DIZDAR

THE VICTORIANS had a passion for lace and flowers. This frame captures that quality, creating an impression of faded glory with lots of detail. It is easy to do, and uses up small pieces of old lace, too delicate for everyday use.

Decorate an old picture frame which has been chipped or marked, buy a cheap wooden frame, or make up a frame from simple mouldings using the instructions on pages 18-19.

~

MATERIALS AND EQUIPMENT

- *lace* ● *small, flat frame*
- *silk flowers* ● *green, coral-pink and cream-coloured emulsion paints* ● *fabric glue*
- *glue gun* ● *spray acrylic varnish* ● *2.5 cm (1 in) paintbrush* ● *5 mm (¼ in) paintbrush*
. . . . . .

1 Using fabric glue, stick strips of lace on to the four sides of the frame, cutting the corners at an angle of 45 degrees to give a neat finish.

2 Arrange a few silk flowers and leaves on the corners of the frame, and glue them in place, using a glue gun as it sticks securely and rapidly.

3 Paint the whole frame, back and front - although not the flowers - with dark green emulsion paint. You do not have to be too careful with the paintbrush: a little dark green on the flowers will not matter. Once the green has dried, paint the flowers in a coral-pink colour.

4 When the paint is completely dry, highlight everything with cream paint, brushing it gently over the top with a dry brush.

5 Finish with a coat of acrylic spray varnish. This will protect the frame and give the whole piece a gentle lustre.

GARDEN OF EDEN

LOU GRAY

INSPIRED BY THE COLOURFUL ceramic candlesticks and Day-of-the-Dead artefacts of Mexico, this papier mâché frame is both inexpensive and great fun to make. Elaborate skills or equipment are not required: only patience is needed to wait for everything to dry in between stages.

As with most papier mâché projects, you will need to have ready plenty of newspaper, torn into tiny pieces. Keep the pieces quite small (about 12 mm/ ½ in works well for a project of this size).

～

MATERIALS AND EQUIPMENT

- *simple wooden frame* • *clay*
- *petroleum jelly* • *newspaper strips* • *PVA glue*
- *masking tape* • *white emulsion paint* • *coloured acrylic paints* • *varnish*
- *craft knife* • *sandpaper*
- *12 mm (½ in) paintbrush*
- *detailing paintbrush*

......

1 Mould the clay into shape, and press on to the wooden frame to form the basic shape of the trees.

2 Build up the clay to create the serpent and woman. Keep the shapes fairly simple, as a certain amount of detail will be lost when the papier mâché is applied. Apply a layer of petroleum jelly all over the clay.

3 Make a watery PVA solution (resembling the consistency of single cream) and soak the paper strips for at least three hours. This makes them really pliable. Cover the clay shape with one layer of paper strips, making sure you overlap the strips as you work. Leave this first layer of papier mâché to dry for around 12 hours before repeating with another layer. Leave the second layer to dry for at least as long as the first.

4 Using a sharp craft knife, cut the papier mâché from the frame to give you a paper shell. Do this gently and gradually: although the papier mâché is quite strong, you do not want it to split. Remove all clay from the frame and inside the paper shell. Glue the shell back on the frame, using masking tape to hold it in place while the glue dries. When dry, remove the masking tape and apply a layer of papier mâché around the edge of the shell to help it blend into the frame.

5 Sand the whole piece down and paint with a coat of white emulsion. Leave to dry.

6 Decorate the frame using the fine paintbrush and a selection of acrylic colours. Keep the colours bold and strong. When the paint is completely dry, protect the frame with a coat of matt or satin varnish.

FABRIC FRAME

BARBARA DIZDAR

Use modern technology to create a very individual and personal frame. Any drawing, photograph or collage can be printed on to a T shirt or cotton fabric in half an hour by visiting a specialised photo image or copying bureau (see Suppliers on pages 94-95). You can then see your own personalized image transformed into a picture frame - a completely unique gift.

~

MATERIALS AND EQUIPMENT

- *flat frame no larger than 15 x 25 cm (6 x 10 in)*
- *magazine cut-outs*
- *family photographs* • *paper*
- *paper glue* • *white 100 per cent cotton fabric about 23 x 32 cm (9 ¼ x 12 ¼ in)*
- *cardboard* • *wadding*
- *fabric glue* • *calico or cotton fabric* • *cotton fabric in contrast colour* • *contact adhesive (optional)* • *scissors*
- *craft knife*

. . . . . .

1 Take the measurements of the outer edge of the basic frame and add 2 cm (¾ in) all round. Make the same allowance for the inner edge of the frame. Create a collage from magazine cut-outs and family photographs, sticking them on to a piece of plain paper, allowing for a space in the centre, and remembering that during the printing process the collage can be reduced or enlarged. Take the collage and cotton fabric to a photo image bureau where your image can be printed on to the cotton fabric.

2 Remove the backing from the frame and lay the front of the frame on to the cardboard. Draw around it, both inside and out. Cut this out with a craft knife. Place the wadding on top of the cardboard and trim it with scissors. Stick the wadding on to the cardboard with fabric glue.

3 Cover the padded cardboard with calico, turning about 1.5 cm (⅝ in) to the back and gluing it in place with fabric glue. Take care when cutting the central section that you snip into the corners for a neat finish. Unless you are very fortunate, you will discover that the calico does not quite cover the corners, and a small piece of wadding is revealed. To cover this, snip a small triangle of the final printed fabric and glue it over the wadding on each of the corners. Set to one side.

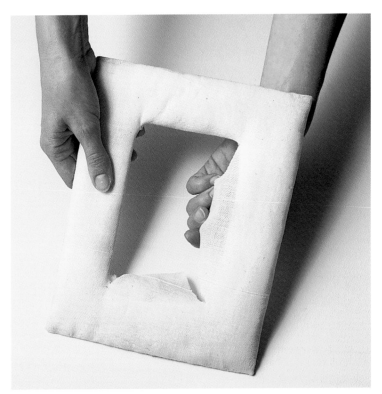

4 Take the contrast fabric, and cover the basic frame, working from the back, so that the edges turn on to the front. Glue down neatly into the recess.

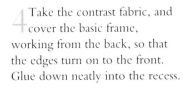

5 Now cover the padded cardboard frame with the final printed fabric in the same way as step 3. Stick this frame to the basic frame with contact adhesive or fabric glue. Here, the oval mount is padded and covered with contrast fabric to complement the overall design.

GILDED CLOCK

BARBARA DIZDAR

THIS CLOCK GIVES YOU A CHANCE to experiment with gold leaf and gesso. The methods and materials date back to the earliest Byzantine icons.

The 'size granules' are made from natural sources, such as the bone and skin of animals. This is the glue that was used in the old fresco painting 2,000 years ago. Gesso is merely white chalk ground very fine, and the glue size is mixed with it to fix it to the wall or other surface, just as we use acrylic glue today. All of these products are available from specialist outlets (see Suppliers on page 94).

This modern, bold design seemed an ideal showpiece for such an old method of decoration.

~

MATERIALS AND EQUIPMENT

• *12 mm (½ in) MDF about 46 cm (18 ½ in) square* • *25 x 25 cm x 6 mm (10 x 10 x ¼ in) MDF* • *glue size granules* • *gesso* • *gold leaf or imitation gold leaf* • *gold leaf size* • *2 'D' rings* • *shellac or white polish* • *black spray gloss paint* • *contact adhesive* • *clock mechanism* • *four glass flat marbles* • *mixing bowl* • *spoon* • *gold leaf brush (optional)* • *pencil* • *card for template* • *compass* • *ruler* • *drill* • *jigsaw* • *sandpaper* • *spatula* • *4 cm (1 ½ in) paintbrush* • *12 mm (½ in) screws* • *screwdriver*
. . . . . .

1 Mix up two tablespoons of size granules with water to a ratio of 1:4. Leave to stand overnight.

2 Using the pencil and ruler, divide the 12 mm (½ in) MDF into 4 equal squares. Make sure they are all square and true. To make the template, enlarge the pattern on page 93 and transfer to a piece of firm card. Place the right angle of the template at the inner corner of the first square and draw around it. Repeat this on each square until you have the basic clock shape. Cut out the shape with a jigsaw.

3 Place the compass point in the centre of the clock shape (using the pencil lines as your guide) and draw a circle 20 cm (8 in) in diameter. Drill a hole inside the circle: this will give you an access point for the jigsaw. Now cut out the circle. Sand the shape well.

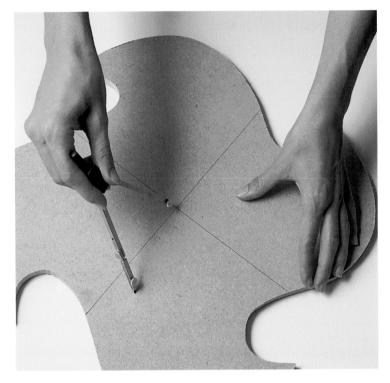

4 Mix 8 parts hot water to 1 part of the prepared glue size and allow it cool. Place approximately 1 cup of gesso powder into a bowl and add the warm size until the mixture is a creamy, pouring consistency. Using a paintbrush, apply a generous coat of this mixture all over the shape, then smooth it over with a spatula, rather as if you were icing a cake. Leave it to dry overnight, then sand down well. You should repeat this process two or three more times to give you a completely smooth, absorbent surface. (As the size cools, it begins to turn to jelly. Simply reheat it when you are ready to use it again.)

5 Apply a coat of gold size and leave to dry. Apply a second coat and while this is still tacky, cut out some strips of gold leaf to cover the edges of the shape. Press the gold leaf on to the shape, using the tissue paper supplied with the leaf to help press it into place. As you should never touch gold leaf, it is worth using a soft brush to manoeuvre it. Practise this technique first on a scrap of wood.

6 Follow the same guidelines to apply sheets of gold leaf to the top of the shape. Try to place the sheets edge to edge, but if they do overlap you can brush away the excess later. Leave the gilded piece to dry overnight, then brush away any surplus pieces of gold leaf.

7 If you are using real gold leaf, you can now burnish the gold. This clock uses imitation gold leaf which is much brighter in colour but widely used and much more affordable. This may tarnish, so it needs a coat of white polish or in this case, a coat of shellac, which dulls the brassy, golden colour.

8 To make the clock face, use a compass to mark out a 21 cm (8 ½ in) circle in the 6 mm (¼ in) MDF. (Make sure you mark the centre point well with the point of the compass, as this will help you later when inserting the clock mechanism.) Cut out the circle with a jigsaw and sand it thoroughly. Spray with black gloss paint. Coat each glass flat marble with gold size and cover with scraps of gold leaf. Fold a large piece of paper into four; unfold, and use this to help you position the gold marbles at the four points of the clock (12, 3, 6 and 9).

9 Glue and screw the face into place from the back, adding one or two D rings to hang the clock by. Drill a hole in the centre of the clock to accommodate the central spindle of the clock mechanism. Finish fitting the mechanism as instructed by the manufacturer.

PATTERNS

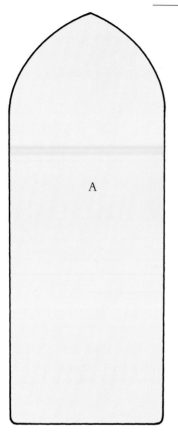

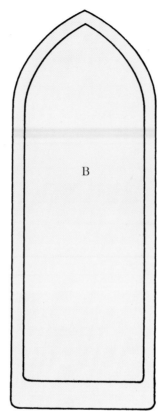

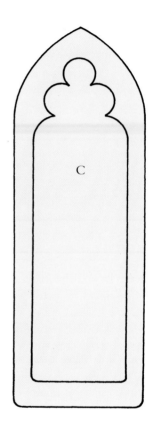

A

B

C

Triptych page 34

Use a photocopier to enlarge these patterns. Scale 1:5

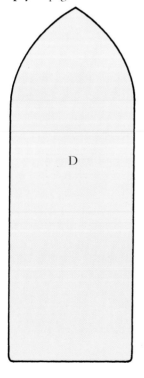

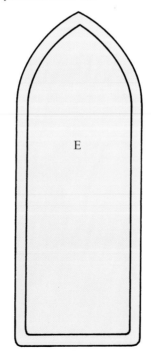

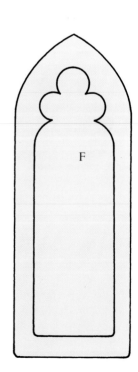

D

E

F

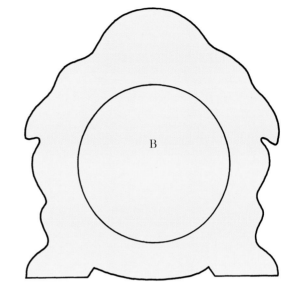

Baroque Mirror page 56

Use a photocopier to enlarge these patterns. Scale 1:20

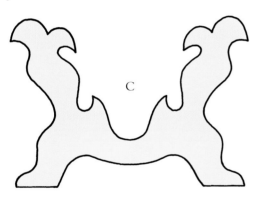

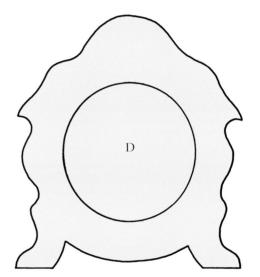

Harvest Mice page 52

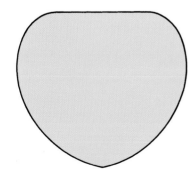

Use a photocopier to enlarge this pattern. Scale 1:4

Gilded Clock page 86

Use a photocopier to enlarge this pattern. Scale 1:5

SUPPLIERS

UNITED KINGDOM

L CORNELISSEN & SON LTD
105 Great Russell Street, London WC1B 3RY
Tel: 0171 636 1045
(manufacturers and retailers of materials for
painters, pastellists, gilders and printmakers)

SIMONART
120-150 Hackney Road, London E2 7QS
Tel: 0171 739 3744
(picture moulding specialists and framing suppliers)

EVERGREEN ENTERPRISES
3 Halls Farm Close, Knaphill, Woking, Surrey
GU21 2NR   Tel: 01483 474479
(framing specialists, mail order)

ALEC TIRANTI LTD
27 Warren Street, London W1P 5DG
Tel: 0171 636 8565
(gold leaf and gilding materials)

FRED ALDOUS LTD
PO Box 135, 37 Lever Street, Manchester 1
M60 1UX   Tel: 0161 236 2477
Fax: 0161 236 6075
(general craft supplies, mail order)

SNAPPY SNAPS LTD
Unit 12, Glenthorne Mews,
115 Glenthorne Road, London W6 0LJ
Tel: 0181 741 7474
(photo image bureaux. Branches around the
country.)

LEAD AND LIGHT
35a Hartland Road, London NW1 8DB
Tel: 0171 485 0997
(stained glass suppliers)

SPECIALISTS IN FRAMES

DIZAR
220 West End Lane, London NW6
Tel: 0171 435 6230

TEMPUS STET LTD
Trinity Business Centre, 305 Rotherhithe Street,
London SE16 1EY   Tel: 0171 231 0953

WILDE AT ART
2 Michael Road, London SW6 2AD
Tel: 0171 371 8761

SASHA BOWLES
46-52 Church Road, London SW13 0DQ
Tel: 0181 563 1961

CLAIRE SOWDEN
6 Bramling Avenue, Yateley, Camberley, Surrey
GU17 7NX   Tel: 01252 870334

SUZANNE MALYON
38 Edgehill House, Loughborough Road, London
SW9 7SQ   Tel: 0171 733 2800

ANNE TAYLOR
18 Parfrey Street, London W6 9EN
Tel: 0181 748 9279

REBECCA NEWNHAM MOSAICS
110-116 Kingsgate Road, London NW6 2JG
Tel: 0171 328 6741

SHOELESS JOE LTD
22 Iliffe Yard, Crampton Street, London
SE17 3QA Tel: 0171 701 8624

SOUTH AFRICA
BURMCO
PO Box 668, East London 5200
(glasscutters)

FRAMART
70 Bree Street, Cape Town Tel: (021) 246939
(Stockists of all materials and equipment)

**MOULDINGS & FRAMES INTERNATIONAL
(PTY) LTD**
68 Albert Road, Woodstock Tel: (021) 4485430
(mounting boards and framing equipment,
gilding and lacquering materials, glass)

MSI MOULDING
Unit 18, Gallagher Place, Cnr Suttie Road,
Midrand and Richard Avenue, Midrand,
Johannesburg Tel: (011) 8243209
(mounting board, framing equipment
and glasscutters)

SA PICTURE FRAMING CO (PTY) LTD
15 Shortmarket Street, Cape Town
Tel: (021) 233867
(mouldings board and framing equipment, gilding
and lacquering materials)

SUPREME LARSON & JEWEL
1008 Katrol Avenue, Robertville
Tel: (011) 6745540
(mounting board and framing equipment)

AUSTRALIA
DEAN'S ART
21 Atchison Street, St Leonards, NSW 2065
Tel: (02) 439 4944

FIX–A–FRAME
1925 Logan Road, Upper Mt Gravatt,
Queensland 4122 Tel: (07) 3849 8164

MILFORD FRAMERS ART SUPPLIES
Unit 15b, 190 Swansea (East), East Victoria Park,
Western Australia 6101 Tel: (09) 361 1202

ROBELL FRAMING GALLERY
73 Mackie Road, Mulgrave Road, Mulgrave
Victoria 3170 Tel: (03) 9561 7111

SOMERTON PARK ART SUPPLIES
11 Oaklands Road, Somerton Park,
South Australia 5044 Tel: (08) 294 9290

NEW ZEALAND
AUCKLAND FOLK ART CENTRE
591 Remuera Road, Upland Village, Remuera
Tel: (09) 524 0935

HANDCRAFT SUPPLIES NZ LTD
13-19 Rosebank Road, Avondale
Tel: (09) 828 3636 Fax: (09) 828 9834

MT ROSKILL GLASSWORX
30 Stoddard Road, Mr Roskill
Tel: (09) 629 3132 Fax: (09) 629 0329

WEBSTERS PICTURE FRAMING SUPPLIES
33 Leslie Avenue, Morningside, Auckland
Tel: (09) 846 3971 Fax: (09) 846 2976

INDEX